# 110 Best Scottish Tunes

## volume 1

### Best

with guitar chords

collected by John Canning

Waltons
publishing

## A Note on the Arrangements

In Irish and Scottish dance music playing it is not unusual to start a tune with an introductory upbeat which is not part of the tune and which is not played on repeats, or also if the tune is second or third in a set of tunes. Such notes are indicated in this book with a dashed barline or a backward repeat after the note as illustrated below.

It is also common to finish a tune with a finishing long note or flourish, which is not used in the first pass, and is not part of the tune. Such notes are indicated in this book with a dashed barline after the note as illustrated below.

Music Setting & Arrangement • John Canning

Book alone: Order No. 11AWAL-1386
ISBN No. 978-1-85720-186-4

CD Edition: Order No. 11AWAL-1386CD
ISBN No. 978-1-85720-187-1

Exclusive Distributors:

Waltons Musical Instrument Galleries Ltd.
Unit 6A, Rosemount Park Drive, Rosemount Business Park,
Ballycoolin Road, Dublin 11, Ireland
www.waltonsmusic.com

The James Trading Group
33 Murray Hill Drive, Nanuet, New York, NY 10954, USA
www.thejamestradinggroup.com

1   3   5   7   9   0   8   6   4   2

# contents

## Reels

## Jigs

## Strathspeys

## Miscellaneous

reels

# The Drummer

# Jenny Dang the Weaver

# The Fairy Dance

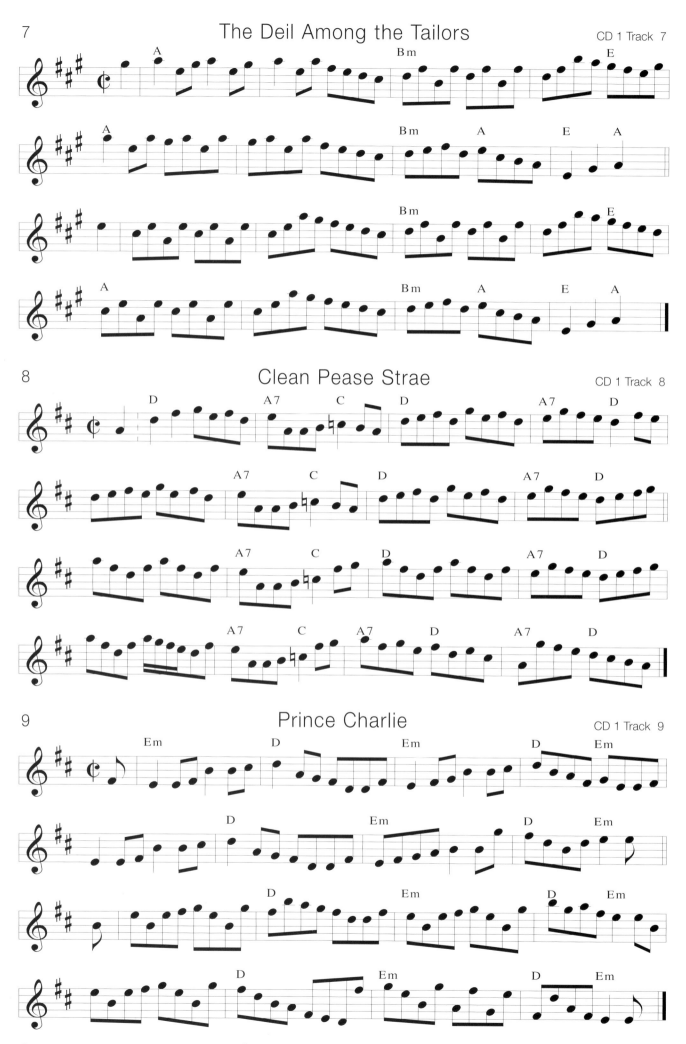

7 The Deil Among the Tailors — CD 1 Track 7

8 Clean Pease Strae — CD 1 Track 8

9 Prince Charlie — CD 1 Track 9

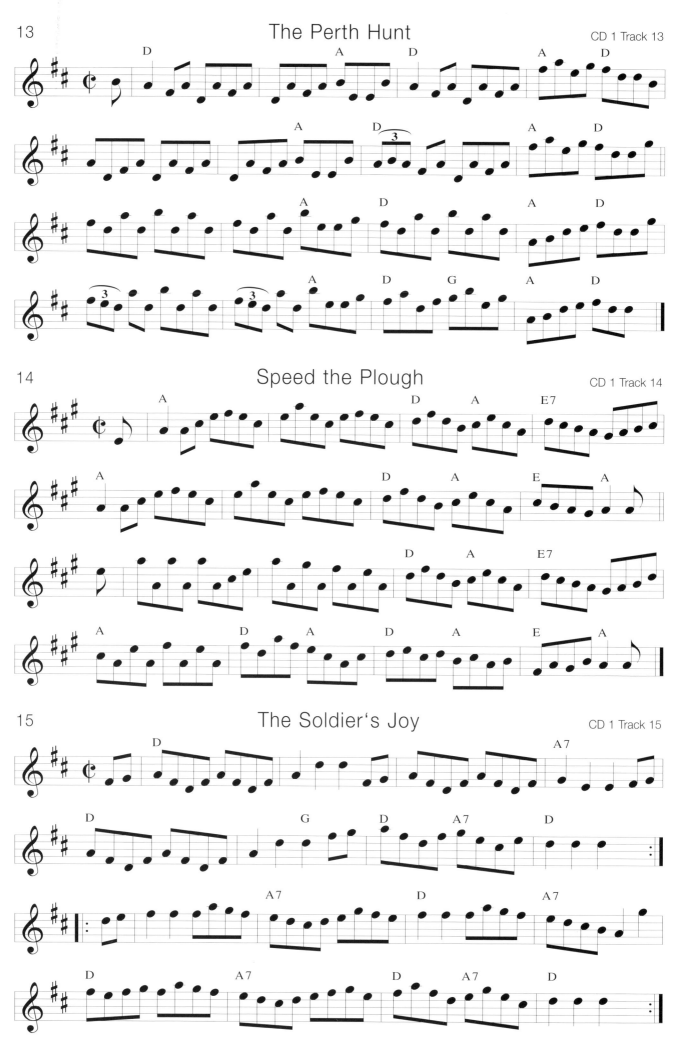

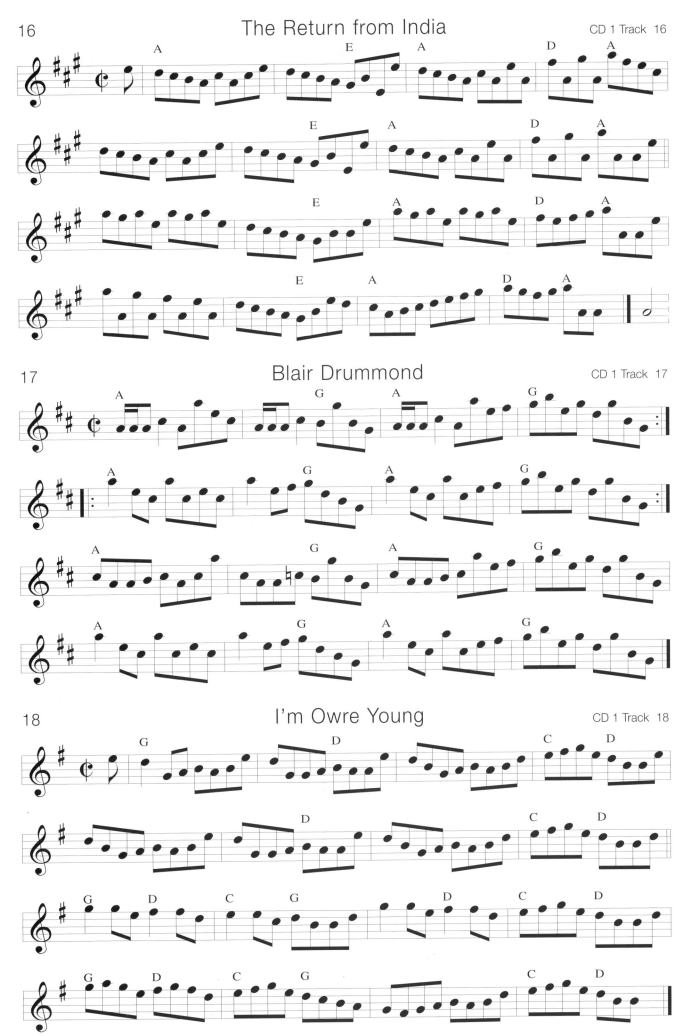

16 The Return from India CD 1 Track 16

17 Blair Drummond CD 1 Track 17

18 I'm Owre Young CD 1 Track 18

# Loch Leven Castle

# Lord MacDonald

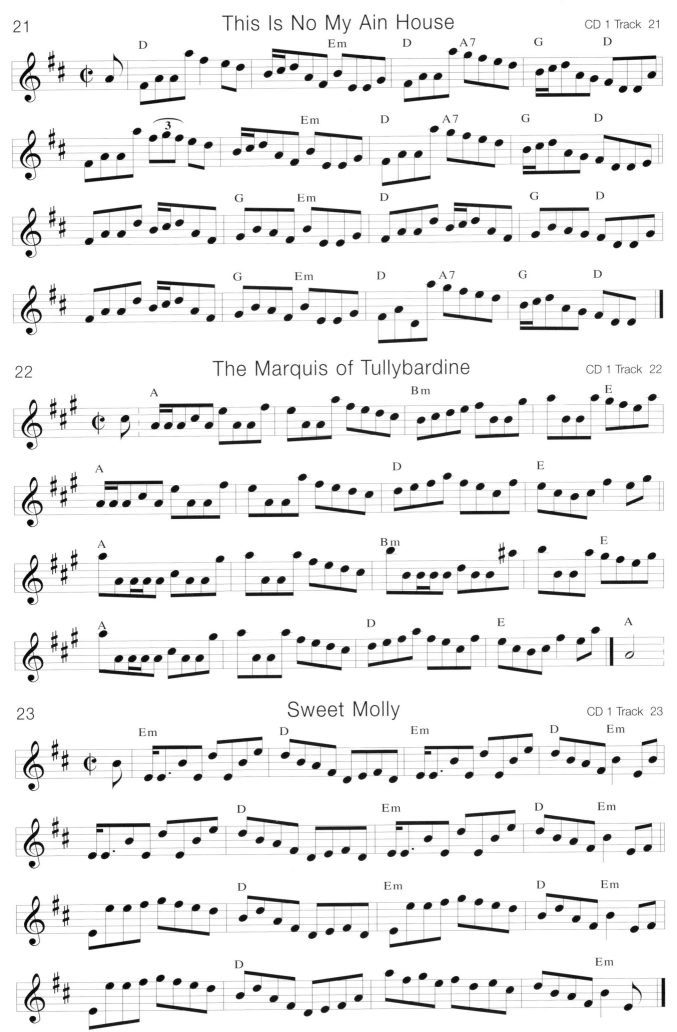

21 **This Is No My Ain House** — CD 1 Track 21

22 **The Marquis of Tullybardine** — CD 1 Track 22

23 **Sweet Molly** — CD 1 Track 23

## Timour the Tartar

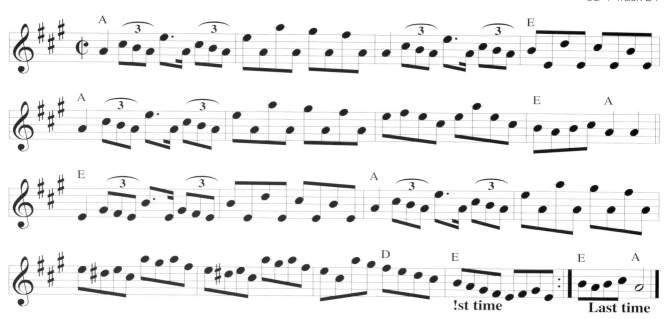

## The Duke of Perth

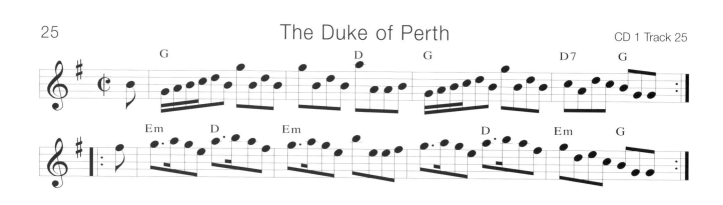

## Captain Keeler

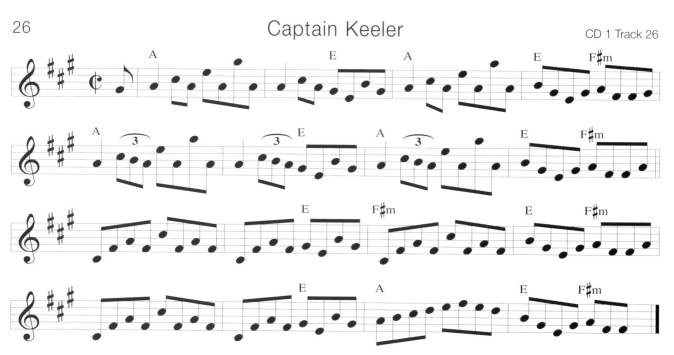

**27**

## Miss Johnston

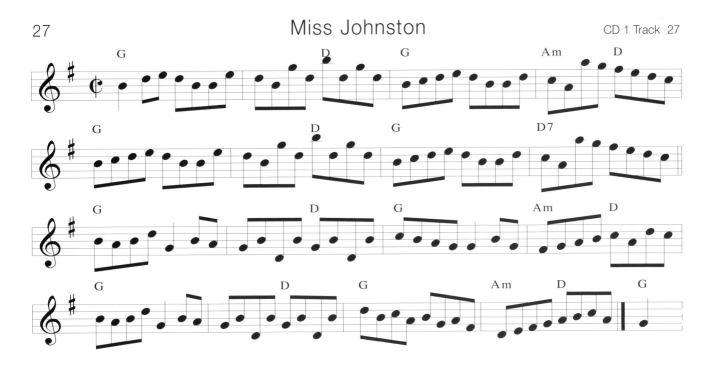

**28**

## Glen Lyon

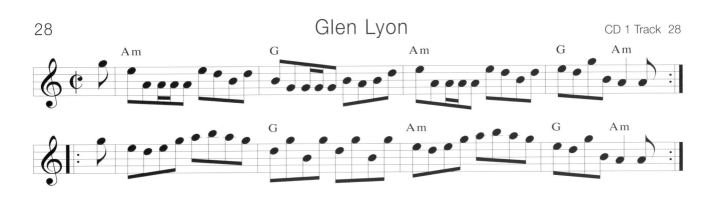

**29**

## Mrs. McLeod

30 Cuttyman and Treladle

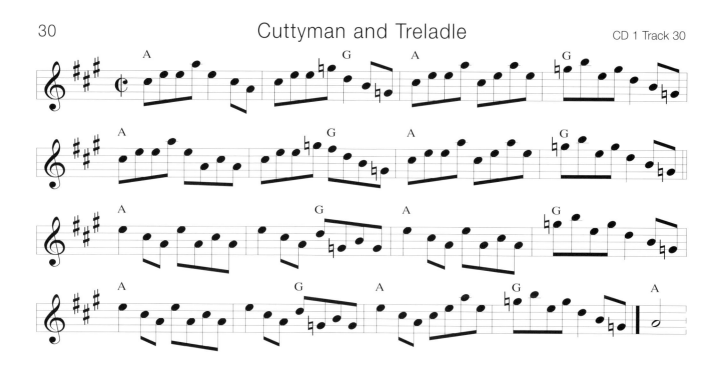

31 Jennie's Bawbee

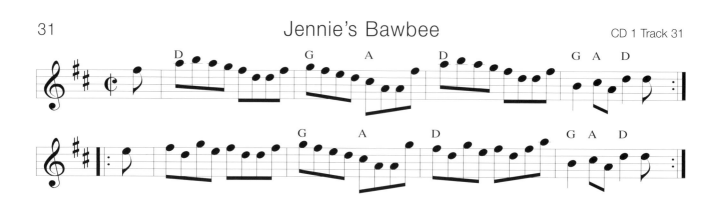

32 The Earl of Dalhousie

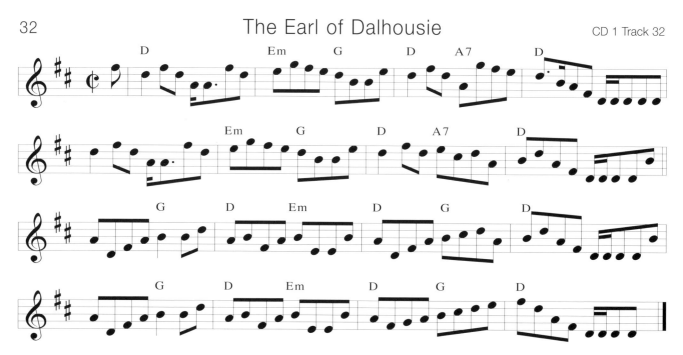

33     Miss Crawford's Reel     CD 1 Track 33

34     Jumping Geordie     CD 1 Track 34

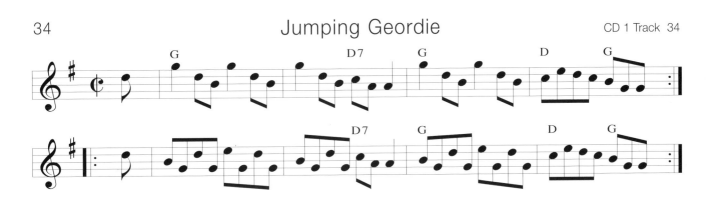

35     Lord Saltoun     CD 1 Track 35

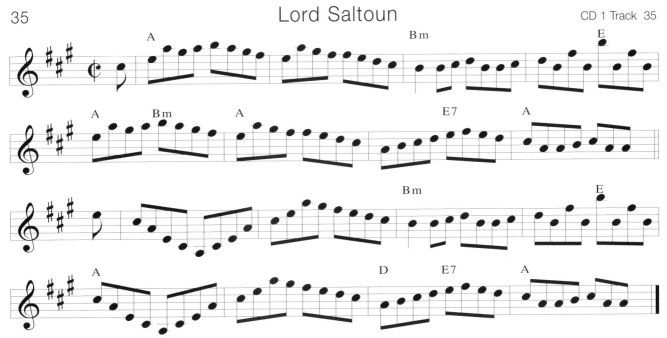

36 Sandy o'er the Lea

CD 1 Track 36

37 Kate Dalrymple

CD 1 Track 37

38 Rachel Rae

CD 1 Track 38

**39** Miss Dumbreck CD 1 Track 39

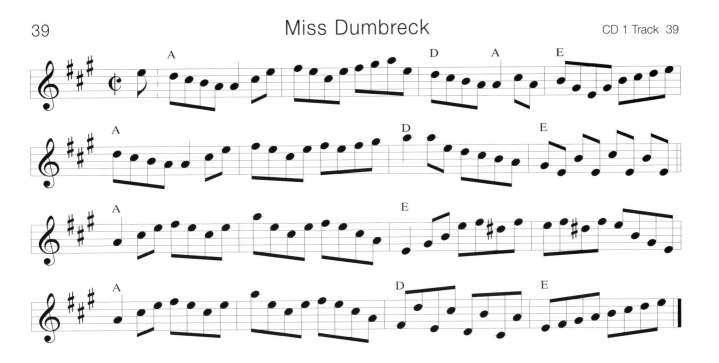

**40** The Pitnacree Ferryman CD 1 Track 40

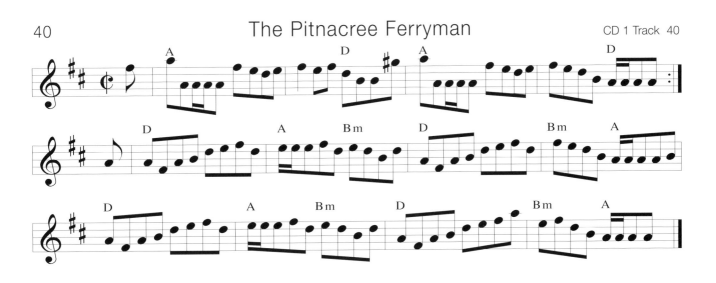

**41** The Perth Assembly CD 1 Track 41

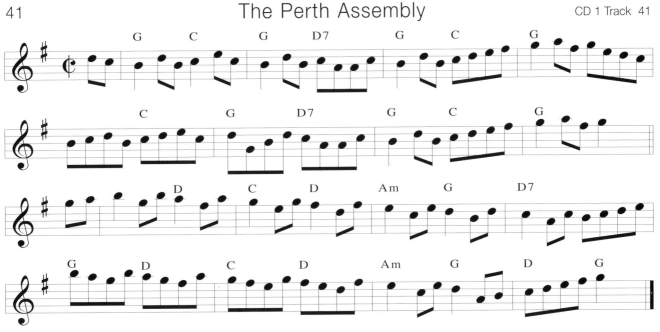

42 Miss Stewart of Fasnacloich

43 Lochiel's Rant

44 Tom Thumb

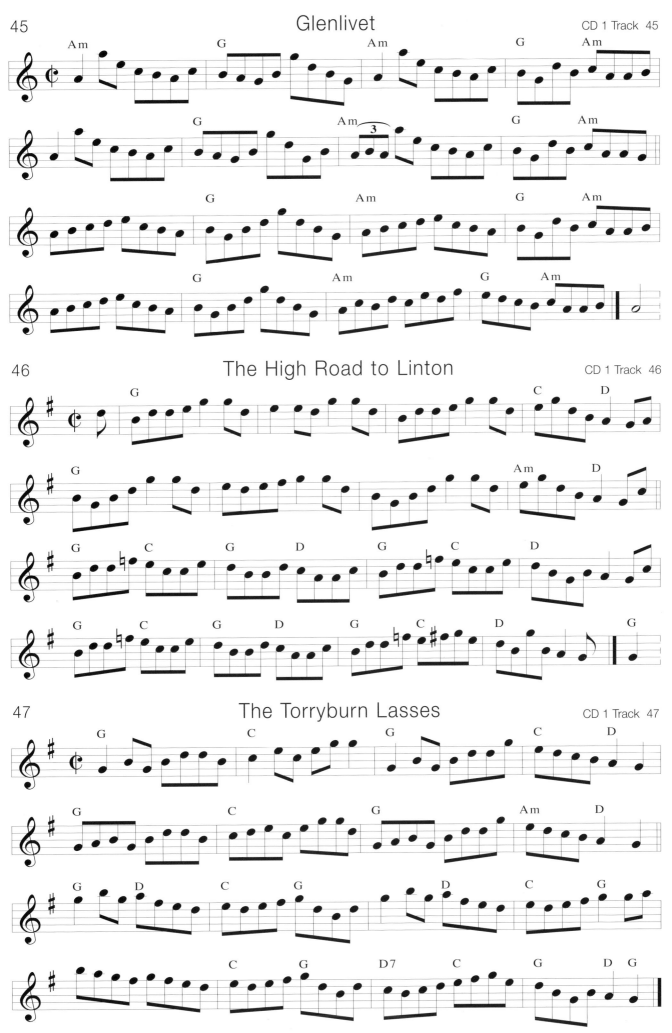

48 The Dashing White Sergeant

CD 1 Track 48

49 Poldwilly Bridge

CD 1 Track 49

50 Glenburnie Rant

CD 1 Track 50

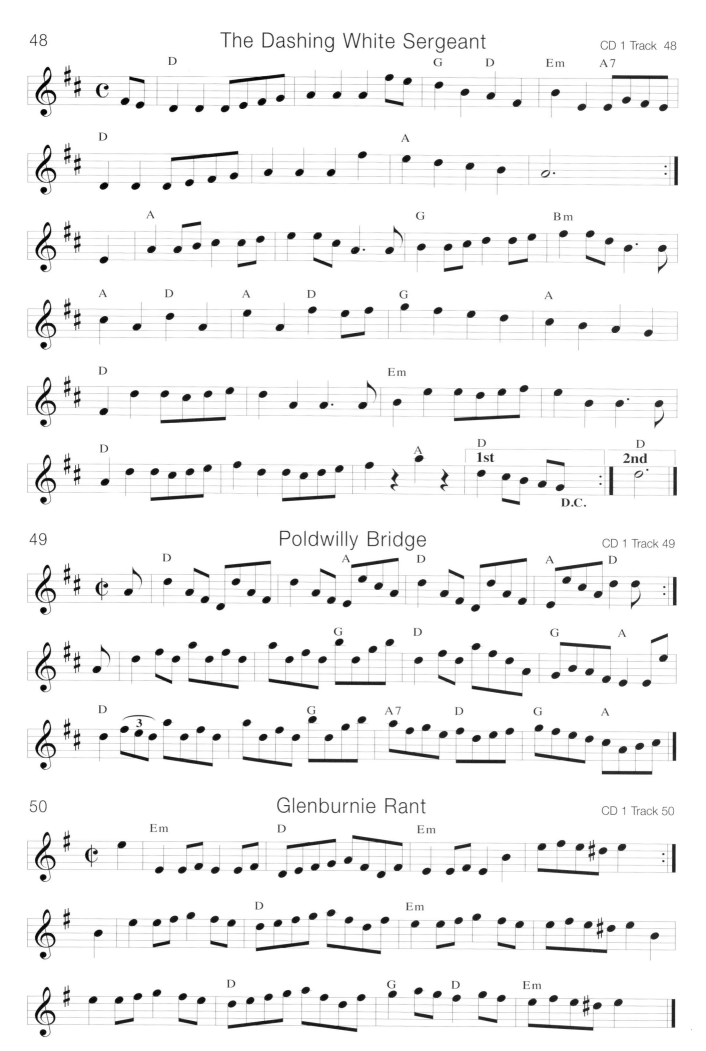

COE RIVER, GLENCOE

## 51 Ane an' Twenty Tam

CD 1 Track 51

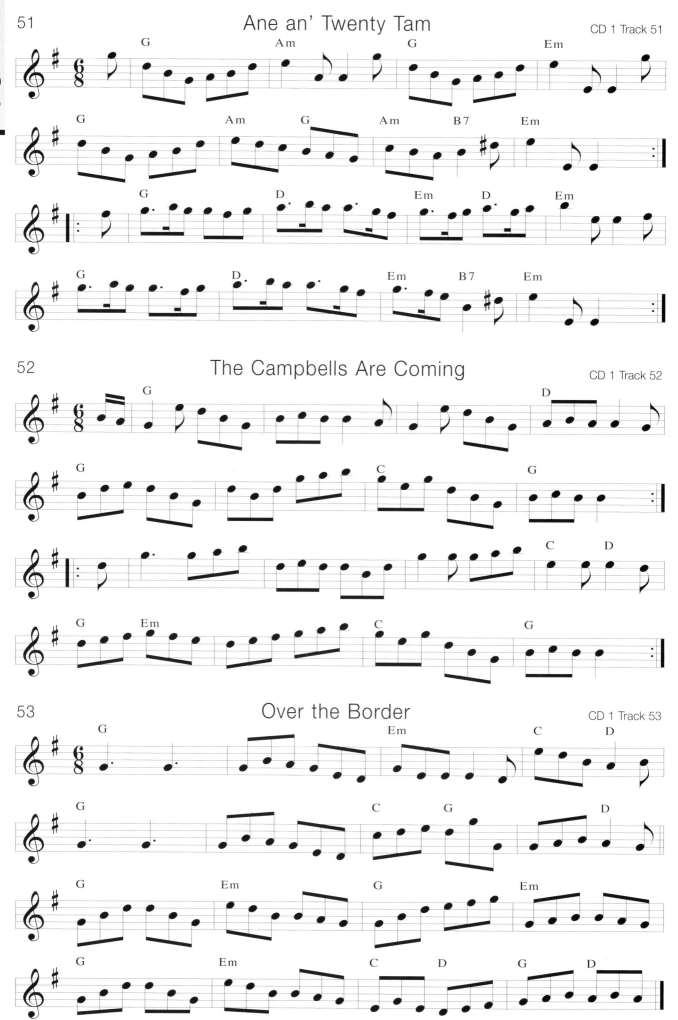

## 52 The Campbells Are Coming

CD 1 Track 52

## 53 Over the Border

CD 1 Track 53

54 Oh, Whistle and I'll Come to You
CD 1 Track 54

55 Argyle Is My Name
CD 1 Track 55

56 Bide Ye Yet
CD 2 Track 1

23

# The Canty Auld Man

# The Lads o' Dunse

# The Gobbie O

CD 2 Track 4

# The Wee Pickle Tow

CD 2 Track 5

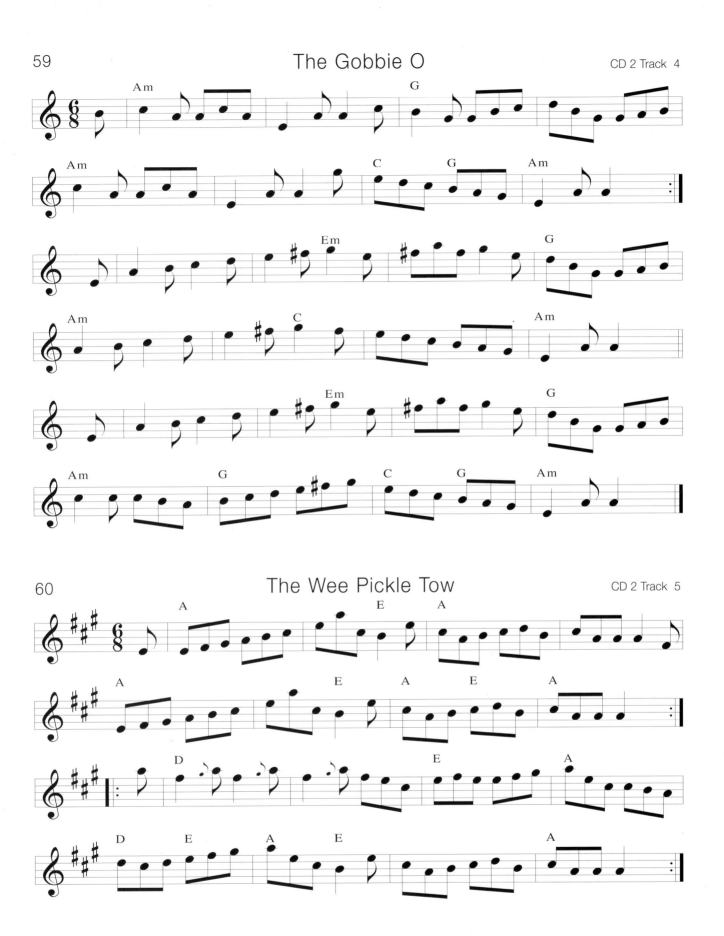

**61**  Kinloch of Kinloch

CD 2 Track 6

**62**  The Lady of the Lake

CD 2 Track 7

**63**  Pibroch o' Donuil Dhu

CD 2 Track 8

Arrangements copyright © 2007 Waltons Publishing

64 Kissed Yestreen

65 I Lo'e Nae a Laddie But Ane

66 There Cam' a Young Man

67 The Hundred Pipers
CD 2 Track 12

68 The Wee Wee Man
CD 2 Track 13

69 The Sailor's Wife
CD 2 Track 14

70    I Lost My Love                    CD 2 Track 15

71    Teviot Bridge                     CD 2 Track 16

72    The Stool of Repentance           CD 2 Track 17

73 Pate Bailie's Jig

74 The Banks of Allan

75 The Atholl Highlanders CD 2 Track 20

76 I'm a Young Man CD 2 Track 21

31

**77** Struan Robertson's Rant — CD 2 Track 22

**78** Stumpie — CD 2 Track 23

**79** The Highlander's Farewell to Ireland — CD 2 Track 24

80 ## Rothiemurchie's Rant

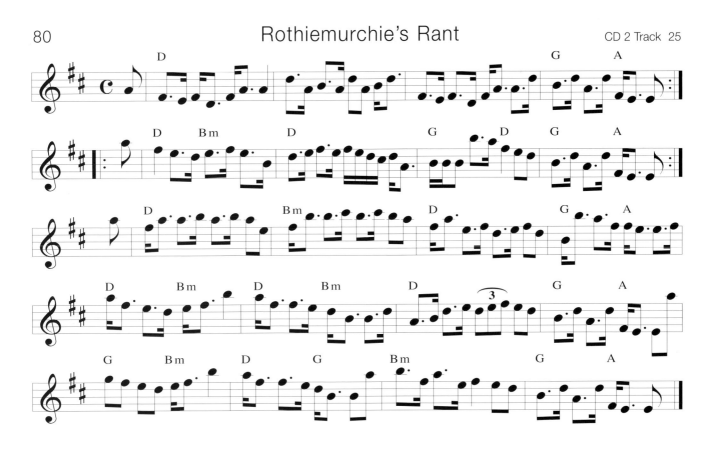

81 ## The Haughs o' Cromdale

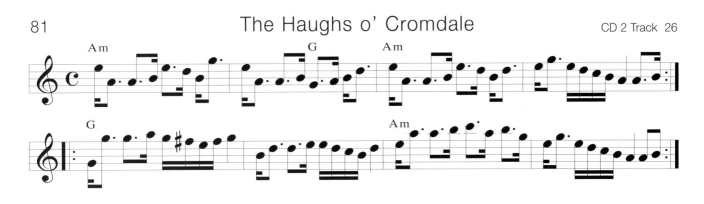

82 ## The Recovery

83 The Marquis of Huntly's Farewell

CD 2 Track 28

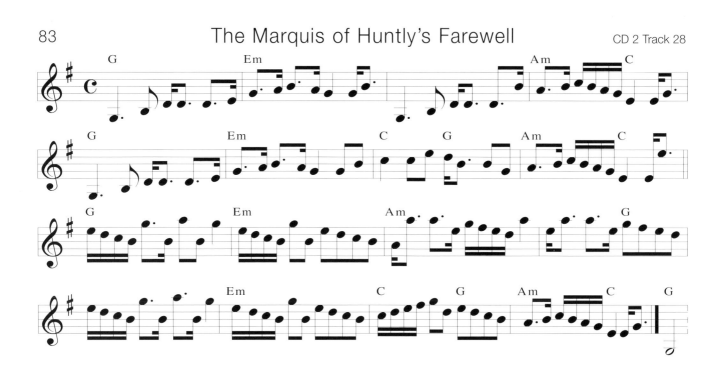

84 The Braes of Tullimet

CD 2 Track 29

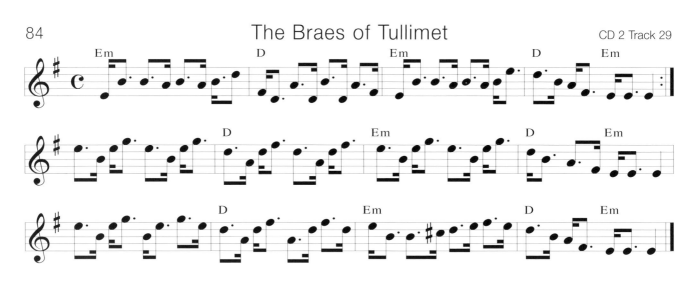

85 Lasses Look Before You

CD 2 Track 30

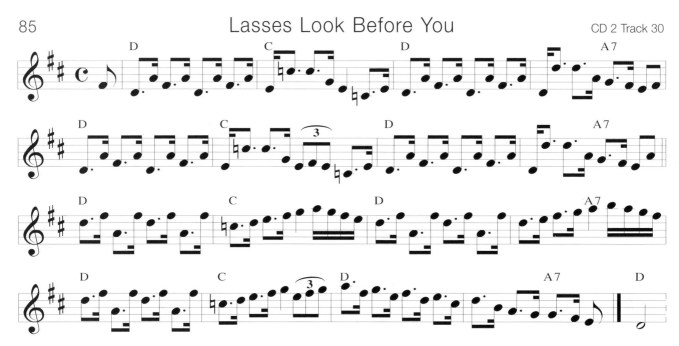

86

## Miss Lyall

CD 2 Track 31

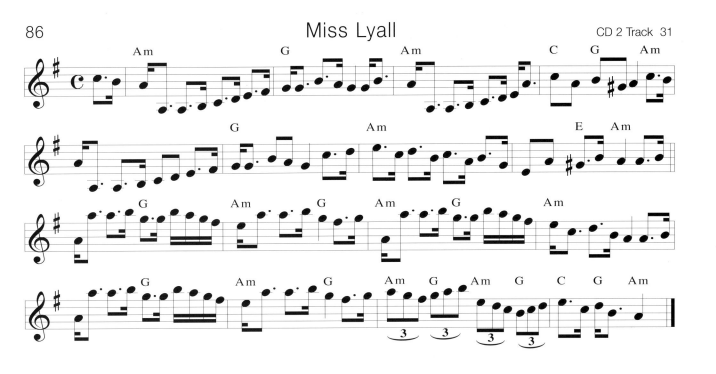

87

## Lady Mary Ramsey

CD 2 Track 32

88

## Neil Gow's Second Wife

CD 2 Track 33

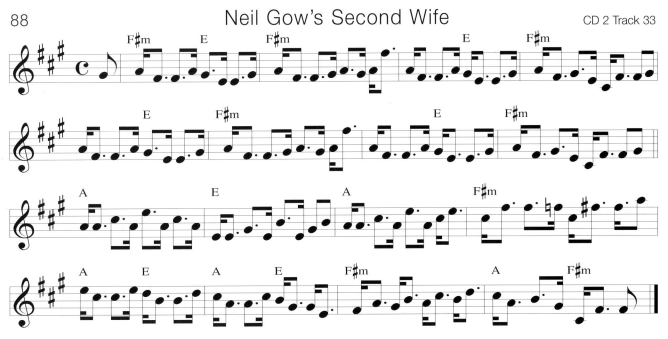

89 Big Kirsty

CD 2 Track 34

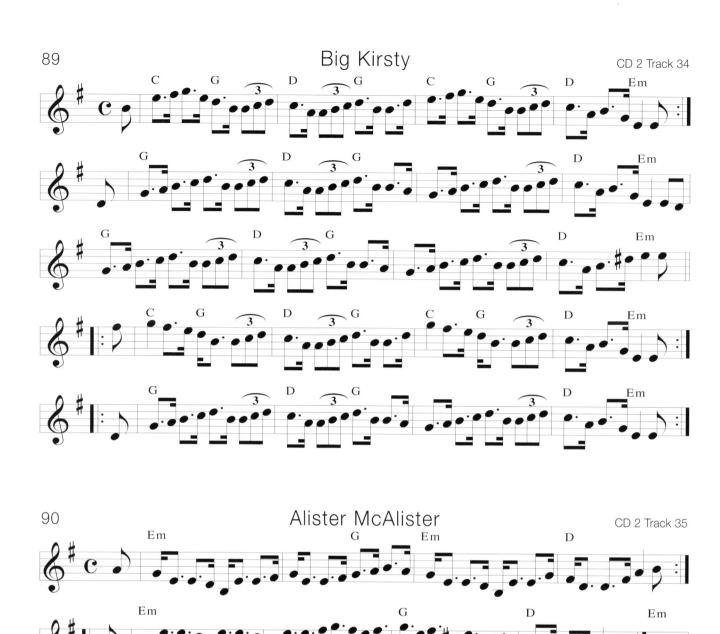

90 Alister McAlister

CD 2 Track 35

91 The Braes of Balquidder

CD 2 Track 36

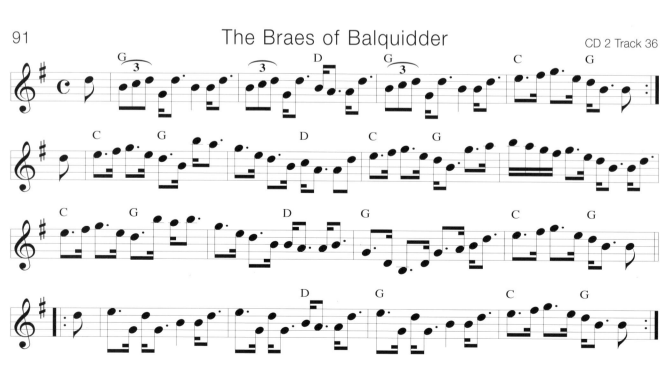

92
## The Marchioness of Huntly

93
## Lady Ann Hope

94
## Smith's a Gallant Fireman

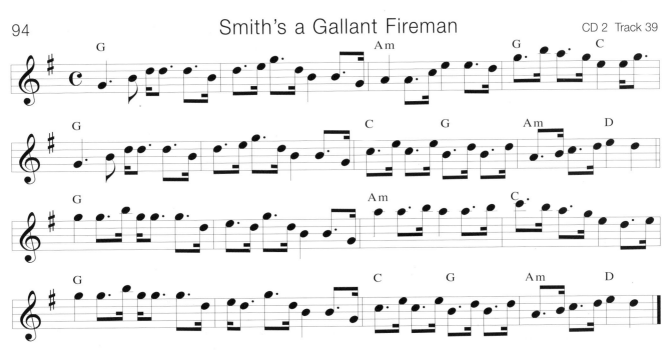

95
# The Atholl Cummers

CD 2 Track 40

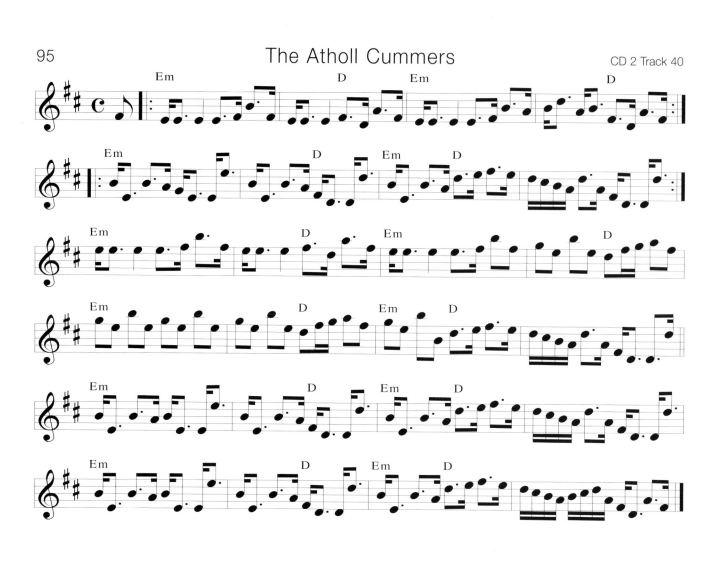

96
# The Duke of Gordon

CD 2 Track 41

97
# Duncan Davidson

CD 2 Track 42

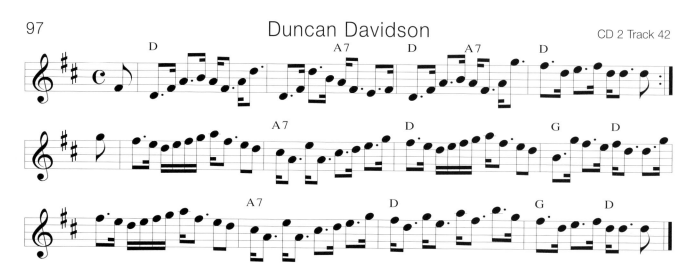

## The Marquis of Huntly's Highland Fling

CD 2 Track 43

## Miss Drummond of Perth

CD 2 Track 44

## Bonnie Mary of Argyll (Air)

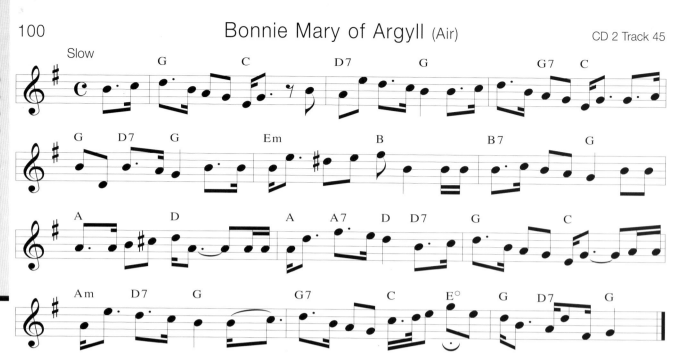

## Coorie Doon (Lullaby)

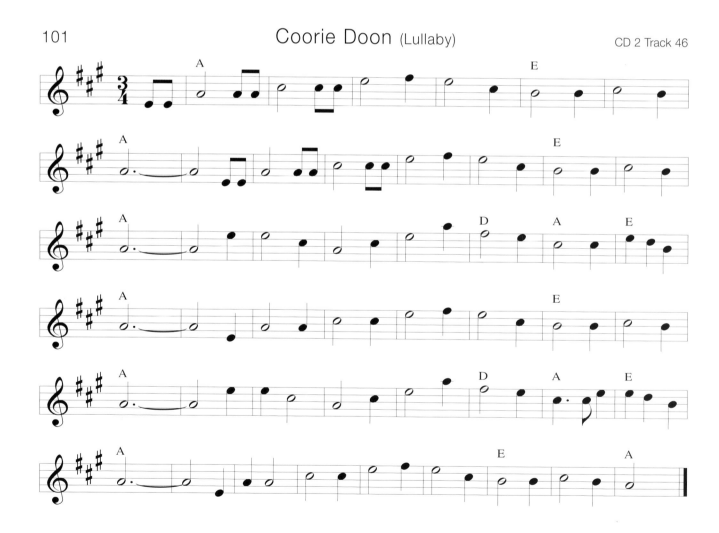

miscellaneous

# Fingal's Cave (Slow March)

# Farewell to Lochaber

# Killicrankie

KILLICRANKIE PASS

105

# The Four Posted Bed

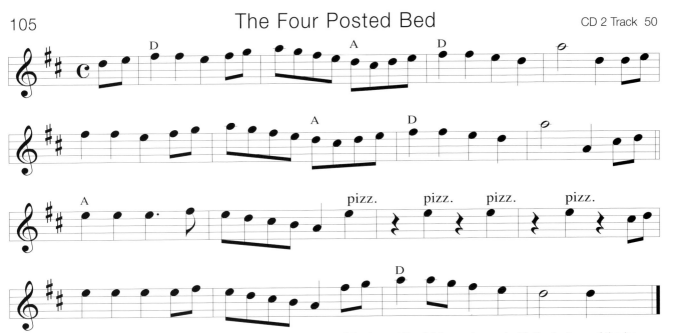

For pizz. the E string is plucked, for the rests the four corners of the top of the fiddle are tapped with the bottom of the bow.
Since this can damage the surface of the fiddle many musicians use alternative means of achieving a similar effect.

106

# Lord Breadalbane's March

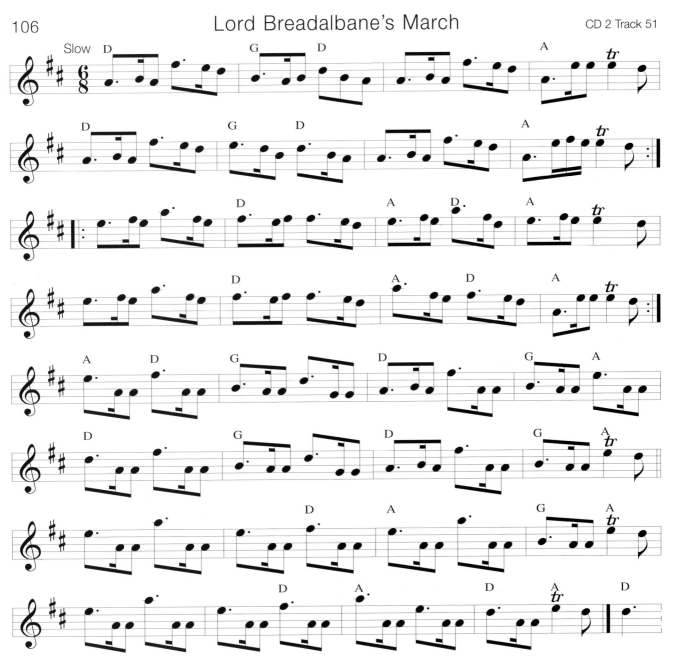

107 Caller Herrin'

108 The White Cockade

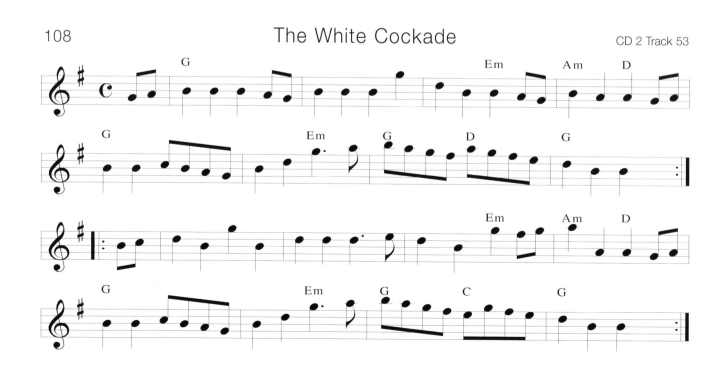

Arrangements copyright © 2007 Waltons Publishing

# The Dancing Scotsman (Schottische)

FINGAL'S CAVE ON THE ISLAND OF STAFFA OFF THE WEST COAST OF SCOTLAND, CONSIDERED TO BE THE OTHER END OF THE GIANT'S CAUSEWAY COUNTY ANTRIM. FINGAL IS THE SCOTS NAME FOR FINN MAC COOL.

# MacGregor's Gathering